WETLANDS

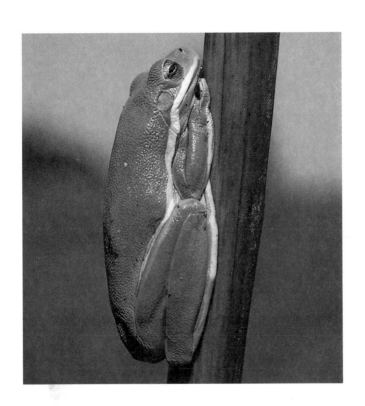

Also by Downs Matthews and Dan Guravich

Arctic Summer
Polar Bear Cubs
Skimmers

WETLANDS

BY DOWNS MATTHEWS
PHOTOGRAPHS BY DAN GURAVICH

SIMON & SCHUSTER BOOKS FOR YOUNG READERS
Published by Simon & Schuster
New York   London   Toronto   Sydney   Tokyo   Singapore

SIMON & SCHUSTER BOOKS FOR YOUNG READERS
Simon & Schuster Building, Rockefeller Center
1230 Avenue of the Americas, New York, New York 10020
Text copyright © 1994 by Downs Matthews
Illustrations copyright © 1994 by Dan Guravich
All rights reserved including the right of
reproduction in whole or in part in any form.
SIMON & SCHUSTER BOOKS FOR YOUNG READERS
is a trademark of Simon & Schuster.
Manufactured in the United States of America

10 9 8 7 6 5 4 3 2 1

Library of Congress Cataloging-in-Publication Data
Matthews, Downs. Wetlands / by Downs Matthews ;
photographs by Dan Guravich. p. cm.
Summary: Describes different types of wetlands and the
animals and plants that are found there. 1. Wetland
ecology—Juvenile literature. 2. Wetlands—Juvenile literature.
[1. Wetlands. 2. Wetland Ecology. 3. Ecology.]
I. Guravich, Dan, ill. II. Title. QH541.3.M3M38 1993
574.5'26325—dc20 93–3439 CIP
ISBN: 0–671–86562-5

Page 13, bottom: photograph courtesy of
Louisiana Wildlife & Fisheries

*In memory of biologist John Lynch,
whose pioneering research and innovative
thinking led to the creation of wetlands
sanctuaries along the entire coast
of the Gulf of Mexico.*

A wetland is...

a shallow pond on a prairie, where ducks paddle among bulrushes and red-winged blackbirds call.

a still swamp shaded by cypress trees, where crayfish burrow in mud and alligators swim.

a saltwater marsh, where baby shrimps hide in eelgrass and great blue herons wade.

a bog in a wooded valley, where beavers build their lodges and green moss grows thick.

a sea of grass, where rainwater flows slowly toward the ocean and deer browse and muskrats raise their families.

▽ White-tailed deer

△ Great blue heron

Muskrat ▽

Wetlands are everywhere. A wetland is just a low spot in the land where water collects and stays. Without water there can be no life. Wetlands make a cradle for plants and animals that are important to people. That is why wetlands are important to all living things.

We call wetlands by many different names. The most common name is *marsh*. Marshes are wet grasslands. Some marshes are made by fresh water and some by salt water. Some marshes are made by brackish water, where fresh and saltwater mix.

When water floods a place where trees grow, we call it a *swamp*. Some of the world's marshes and swamps are hundreds of years old.

Freshwater marshes are nourished by rain and melting snow. Marsh plants catch and hold soil so that it does not wash away. As rain falls, marshes slow its flow to the sea. In that way, marshes help to prevent harmful floods. They allow water to seep into the earth, where it flows into wells that give us drinking water.

Soil helps keep the marsh healthy. Dead leaves and stems of plants rot in the marsh and provide food for plants and animals.

▽ Golden club

Water in saltwater marshes comes from the ocean. Saltwater marsh plants soften the force of winds and waves and reduce damage from hurricanes. Their roots hold soil in place so the sea cannot wash it away.

In all wetlands, life begins with water-loving plants.

Some water plants are too small for people to see. These tiny plants find nourishment in the water. They serve as food for small animals.

Wetlands are home to larger plants, too. Sawgrass grows in freshwater marshes. So do water lilies, bulrushes, and cypress trees. They are all plants that cannot live in salty soil.

▽ Water lily

△ Sea oats   Cordgrass ▽

In a saltwater marsh, cordgrass thrives. Glasswort, sea oats, and black mangroves grow by the water's edge. These plants have all learned how to grow in salty soil.

Plants clean up dirty water that flows into wetlands. A plant takes up water through its roots. The plant's roots and leaves filter out poisons. This makes the water safe for people and animals to drink.

Tiny water animals feed on even smaller water plants. In turn, the animals become food for young shrimps, fish, tadpoles, and shellfish. When these animals grow up, they mate and lay their eggs in the marsh. They lay lots and lots of eggs because fish and birds eat most of them. Some eggs escape being eaten. They hatch, and the babies grow up to be adults.

Many finfish and shellfish use the saltwater marsh as a nursery for their young. Their eggs hatch in the marsh, safe from animals that would eat them. The hatchlings leave the marsh's sheltering waters when they are large enough to survive in the open sea.

People depend on fish for food. Most of the seafood we eat begins life in wetlands. If wetlands disappear, our favorite seafood will disappear, too.

△ Blue crab

Ghost crab ▽

Insects depend on wetlands. Many spend part of their lives in the water and part of their lives in the air. Although insects can be a nuisance to people, birds and fish need bugs as food. Some insects help plants to make seeds. They take pollen from one flower and put it on another flower. Then seeds can form to make new plants. Wetlands could not survive without insects.

△ Zebra and buckeye butterflies carry pollen to wetland flowers so that seeds can form. (The zebra butterfly is on top.)

△ To catch flying insects, the golden-silk spider spins a round web between two reed stems.

△ A little goldenrod spider has caught a bluebottle fly by pretending to be a yellow flower.

After mating, the female grasshopper buries clumps of eggs in soft soil where they will hatch. △

Almost all water and wading birds nest in or near marshes. They build their nests with the leaves and twigs of marsh plants.

One of America's largest and rarest birds is the whooping crane. Whooping cranes stand nearly five feet tall. They have a wingspread of almost eight feet and weigh twenty pounds. Their whooping call is so loud, you can hear it three miles away. In summer pairs of cranes build nests in freshwater marshes in western Canada. They raise one chick, sometimes two. In early October, when the chicks have grown their feathers and can fly, the families leave their Canadian wetlands. They fly south all the way to a marsh on the coast of Texas. There they feed all winter on crabs, fish, and snails.

Thousands of whooping cranes once lived in the marshes of Texas and Louisiana. When farmers drained the marshes to plant crops, the cranes had no place to go. Most of them died. Just in time, people saved some wetlands for the cranes. Fewer than two hundred whooping cranes remain alive in the wild today.

While whooping cranes are scarce, there are more red-winged blackbirds in North America than any other kind of bird. Each year millions of red-winged blackbirds fly south from northern marshes. They spend the winter eating insects and seeds in southern wetlands. In February they fly north again. In summer they build nests among the bulrushes. Then they mate and lay eggs. The parents may raise two or even three broods of chicks in one summer.

With its long legs, the great egret can wade in shallow wetland waters and hunt for food. ▷

▽ Red-winged blackbird

Many fish-eating birds use wetlands. Brown pelicans stay near the ocean, where there are plenty of fish to eat. But during winter months, when brown pelicans mate, they look for a marsh near shore where they can build their nests. They like to nest on marshy islands where their eggs are safe from coyotes and raccoons. Each pair of pelicans makes a nest on top of a clump of grass. The male brings sticks and stems and puts them on the nest. He builds it up high so that the female's eggs won't get wet when the tide comes in. When a flock of brown pelicans finds a good place to nest, they will go there year after year.

△ Green tree frog

△ Bullfrog

Birds share wetlands with snakes, lizards, frogs, and turtles. The green anole, a common lizard, lives on tree branches and grass stems. The anole can change color. On green leaves, it turns green. On brown tree bark, it turns brown. Anoles change color to hide from birds that eat them. This disguise also helps them surprise insects that they eat.

Bullfrogs live in freshwater wetlands. They hide at the water's edge among the leaves of water plants. The bullfrog's croak is deep and loud. It sounds like "jug-o-rum." Some bullfrogs grow so large that they can capture and eat little birds and snakes. But mostly they eat insects and minnows.

While bullfrogs sit in the water, green treefrogs like to sit above it. Treefrogs cling to the stems and leaves of water plants with the help of large pads on their toes. Instead of hopping like most frogs, they walk. The treefrog catches insects with its long, sticky tongue. It has a clear, bell-like call.

Many water-loving snakes live in wetlands. Water snakes are good swimmers. They feed mostly on frogs, minnows, and insects. A few snakes are poisonous, but most are not. Snakes with long narrow stripes, like the blue-striped garter snake, are not poisonous. The common garter snake inhabits every wetland in North America.

Many turtles prefer fresh water, but some live in salty coastal marshes. The diamond–back terrapin feeds on worms, clams, and snails that it finds along the grassy shores of bays and ocean inlets. Once people liked to eat diamondback terrapins. Hunters took so many of them that they became scarce. Laws were passed to protect terrapins.

△ Blue-striped garter snake

△ Diamondback terrapin

The largest reptile in the wetlands is the alligator. A mother alligator makes a kind of haystack out of marsh plants and uses it as a nest in which to lay her eggs. Alligators feed on snakes, turtles, and fish. They also feed on muskrats. If there were no alligators, the muskrats might eat all the marsh plants. That's called an *eat-out*. Without plants the marsh would be destroyed. Then all the muskrats would die. Alligators help to keep that from happening.

△ Nutria

△ Raccoons make their homes in trees near streams and lakes throughout North America.

Along with muskrats, families of nutria live in the marsh. The nutria is a furry mammal from South American wetlands. Long ago a man brought several pairs of nutria to a North American zoo. One day a storm blew down their cage and the nutria escaped. Now nutria live in North American wetlands, too. South Americans call them coypu, which means "water sweeper." Nutria live in holes that they dig into the earth at the water's edge.

Beavers help make marshes. They are builders. They cut down small trees with their big teeth. They drag the trees into a creek. They build a dam of tree trunks and branches, packed with rocks and mud. Behind the dam a pond forms. In the pond beavers build a lodge of tree branches and mud. They live there safe from animals that would like to eat them. The beavers' pond becomes a home for fish. Marsh plants spring up at the water's edge. Slowly a wet-land begins to form.

In winter the leaves of wetland plants die and turn brown. Without green plants to eat, animals there may starve. But if fire burns away the dead leaves, fresh young plants spring up and animals have food again. Fire helps restore the wetland. Fires may start naturally. Sometimes people set fires on purpose to help a new cycle of life begin in the wetlands.

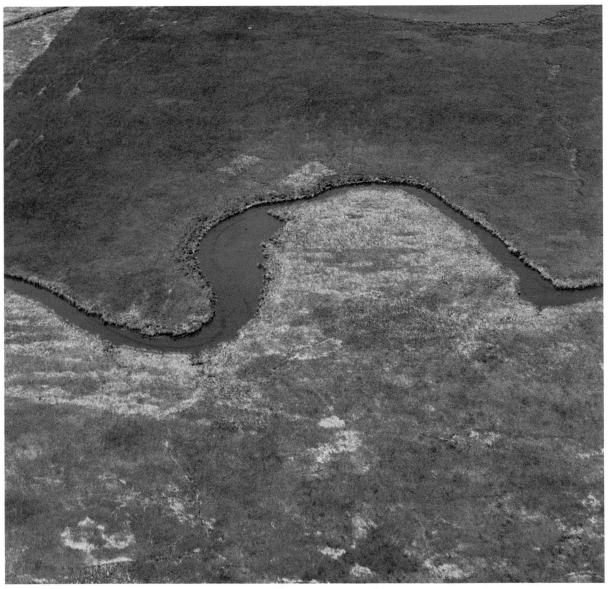

Spring brings new green growth to the burned part of the marsh △

Wetlands are rich in many kinds of life. From the tiny plants too small to see to the giant moose, all kinds of life are important to people. There was a time when we thought wetlands were worthless. Now we know better. Today we help nature rebuild wetlands. We need wetlands because we need what wetlands do.

Wetlands protect us from hunger, thirst, sickness, and storms.

Wetlands give us beautiful scenery with flowering plants and wildlife to enjoy.

Wetlands are a valuable part of our natural world.